T0208472

Be Happy

A Spiritual Journey, Including Insight About ETs and Our Future

LINDA SHRIMPTON

BALBOA.
PRESS
A DIVISION OF HAY HOUSE

Balboa Press books may be ordered through booksellers or by contacting:

Balboa Press
A Division of Hay House
1663 Liberty Drive
Bloomington, IN 47403
www.balboapress.com
1 (877) 407-4847

Print information available on the last page.

ISBN: 978-1-9822-0967-4 (sc)
ISBN: 978-1-9822-0965-0 (hc)
ISBN: 978-1-9822-0966-7 (e)

Library of Congress Control Number: 2018953967

Balboa Press rev. date: 08/06/2018

Contents

Introduction

In my personal journey, in recent times, over a period of about a decade, to learn how is the best way to 'to be me', here is what I 'discovered' along my way ....

Chapter One

Religion/Gnostics

Bible Quotes (Revised Standard Version)

- Ask, and it will be given you; seek, and you will find; knock, and it will be opened to you. For every one who asks receives, and he who seeks finds, and to him who knocks it will be opened. Matt Ch 7v7-8
- Therefore I tell you, whatever you ask in prayer, believe that you receive it, and you will. Mark Ch 11v24
- And this is the confidence which we have in him, that if we ask anything according to his will he hears us. And if we know that he hears us in whatever we ask, we know that we have obtained the requests made of him. 1 John Ch 5v14-15

Gospel of Thomas (discovered in 1945 near Nag Hammadi, ancient codices from AD390)

– suggests that God's Kingdom is inside you

Gospel of Mary Magdalene (discovered in 1896 in a 5th Century papyrus codex)

– Jesus says that the Kingdom is within a person

Secret Book of John (a 2nd Century AD Sethian Gnostic Christian text)

– has in mind to show we have a latent capacity within us, in our hearts and minds, which links us to the divine. This divine capacity for thought is what enables people to encounter the wisdom and knowledge of Jesus in an insightful and creative manner

Buddhism

– "What you think, you become"
– Buddhists have a saying, "If you are facing in the right direction, all you have to do is keep walking", in other words, if your intent is clear about what you want, you'll get there.

The Bible Code (a book by Michael Drosnin)

— Drosnin describes an alleged 'Bible Code', in which
   messages are encoded in Hebrew Bible
— at the end of his book, there is a Bible Code that asks
   along the lines of "Will you change?"

   + To this I believe, will Mankind change its way
      of thinking? In other words, think and believe
      what you want, not what you don't want (Law of
      Attraction?)

— apparently, there is a Bible Code 111 book by M
   Drosnin. In it, it is mentioned that in the Bible
   Codes, Obama would be President!

Chapter Two

Martial Arts

Jim Pritchard

- wrote a book called 'The Warrior Mind'
- in it, he suggests that attentive curiosity, is based on your own life and not on the love of another person and the conviction you have within yourself. To act in your own best interests, for your own well-being and to be awake and be aware to the circumstances that most empower you. Also, to let emotions come and go, not to resist, although not to let hold.
- warrior mind always in the present

+ Abraham teaches to live in the NOW, where everything is attracted to (see Chapter 6. Channelling)
+ Bashar says live in the present, in excitement, where everything is connected (see Chapter 6. Channelling)
+ N Haramein lectures that the 'NIL' place, (in other words present, or now) where everything evolves
+ Ninja warriors speak of 'Void', the nothing from which all things take their form

– Ninja were people who were aware of magnificent powers within themselves

The Spiritual Practices of the Ninja

– These practices have been written about by Ross Heaven, about ordinary people who developed certain skills in order to survive in difficult times
– he suggests skill of stealth
– know what you want
– know yourself

+ "know yourself" is mentioned in the Gnostic material and was inscribed in the forecourt of the Temple of Appollo at Delphi

- do whatever is necessary
- you can have everything
- the point is doing them
- a soul warrior touches the 'void' or 'the 'nothing' from which all things take form
- VOID described as a god-like state
- we must act alone
- if things do not go exactly according to plan, don't fall into the trap of believing you made a mistake, to take it as an inspiration in itself, or an opportunity for further learning and growth, not as failure, but to think what needs to change?

+ reminds me of what Jim Pritchard says in his book 'The Warrior Mind', "The word 'crisis' means 'a situation of extreme danger or difficulty, but also means "a turning point"

+ also reminds me about how the Chinese break down their interpretation of the word 'crisis', which is 'Wei' meaning danger and 'ji' meaning 'opportunity'. This is mentioned in a book called 'Chinese Cinderella' by Adeline Yen Mah

+ also reminds me of Neale Donald Walsch's book, 'When Everything Changes Change Everything', that is, to see crisis as opportunity for change for the better!

+ interesting, again, from the book, 'Chinese Cinderella', it is mentioned that the word for 'intention' in Chinese, is 'hi', meaning 'sound from your heart'.

Chapter Three

New Thought

Guy Ballard, (who used the pen name, Godfre Ray King) meets St Germaine, an Ascended Master, whilst hiking in Northern California and was an American mining engineer who became, with his Wife, founder of the "I AM Activity".

– St Germaine assisted Guy Ballard, in understanding the Ascended Master Law of the 'I AM'

+ St Germaine tells him "Nothing will bless the individual to so great a degree as the conscious understanding of this 'Creative Word'." (From his book, 'The I AM Disclosures'), website, 'bahaistudies.net'

+ reminds me that in the Bible, Moses asks God, who should he say sent him? To which God says "I AM', which apparently means 'causes to become'.
+ also, in the book 'The Moses Code', by James F Twyman, he suggests that 'I AM' is "The Most Powerful Manifestation Tool in the History of the World".
+ Mary Baker Eddy, discoverer and founder of Christian Science, suggests that "I AM, therefore I know" (from her book, 'The Spiritual Writings of Mary Baker Eddy).

Prentice Mulford, was a noted literary humorist, author, early founder of New Thought movement, who coined the term, Law of Attraction

+ he advises that when trying to live to suit others, we shall never suit them, the more we try, the more unreasonable and exacting they become! He suggests the government of your life is a matter which lies entirely with God and yourself and that when your life is swayed and influenced from any other source, you are on the wrong path. The highest and purest love comes to him or her who is most in communion and oneness with the

Infinite Mind, who is ever demanding the Infinite Mind more and more of its wisdom (and are wisely economical of their sympathy for others) and put a great deal of this higher love into themselves, in order to make the most of themselves. The Infinite, as we demand, will give us wisdom and light <u>to know</u> what <u>we owe ourselves</u>

+ he concluded that looking out for yourself as directed by the Infinite is really looking after the other and is the only way to benefit yourself

+ he goes on to say that if we persist in holding to our plan or purpose, 'forces' come nearer and nearer and become stronger and stronger, bringing more and more favourable results (from his book, 'The God in You, Chapter 4 Love Thyself).

Florence Scovel Shinn was an American artist, book illustrator who became a New Thought teacher and metaphysical writer

− her words of advice are

+ substitute faith for fear and that fear is only inverted faith, that is, faith in evil instead of good

+ see clearly one's good and obliterate all mental pictures of evil. In other words, impress the subconscious mind with a realisation of good
+ do not believe you lack, believe in more than enough or plenty
+ faith knows it has already received and acts accordingly
+ you attract the things you give a great deal of thought to
+ when you pray, believe you have it and ACT as if you have already received it
+ expect happiness, success, change for the better, abundance, PREPARE FOR YOUR GOOD. CHANGE YOUR EXPECTANCIES AND YOU CHANGE YOUR CONDITIONS
+ do something to show you expect it to come
+ do not say how you want it done or how it can be done
+ do not let other people 'rock your boat'!
+ success and abundance are states of mind and to live in the now and be wide awake to your opportunities (from her book, 'The Writings of Florence Scovel Shinn).

Charles Haanel, was an American businessman, New
Thought author and philosopher

+ he suggests to be successful, attention must
  invariably be directed to the creative plane, it must
  never seek to deprive. In other words, do. Not to
  wish to take anything away from others, you want
  to create something for yourself and what you
  want for yourself, you are perfectly willing that
  others should have

+ the most desired way is to mentally concentrate
  on the object of your desire. When you are
  concentrating, you are impressing the subconscious. He says that this method produces
  such extraordinary results, many think that
  miracles are being accomplished and that the subconscious mind is a part of the Universal Mind

+ say what you desire, not how you are to obtain it

+ when you come into a realisation of the true
  nature of the "I", you will enjoy a sense of power
  which nothing else can give, because you will
  come to know what you are, who you are, what
  you want and how to get it!

+ if you start something, see it through (even if the
  heavens fall!) Make up your mind to do something,

DO IT! Let nothing, no-one interfere, the "I" in you has determined, the thing is settled, the die is cast, there is no longer any argument

+ you can be what you will to be by imagining/concentrating on what you would like and you will gradually bring the 'thing' nearer to you

+ thought will lead to action, action will develop methods, methods will develop friends, friends will bring about circumstances and finally, materialisation will have been accomplished

+ the law of thought will manifest in form and only <u>one who knows</u> how to be the divine thinker of his own thoughts can ever take a MASTER'S place and speak with authority

+ you must first have the knowledge of your power, second, the courage to dare, third, faith to do

+ if you desire to visualise a different environment, the process is simply to hold the ideal in mind, until vision has been made 'real', giving no thought to persons, places or things, the environment you desire will contain everything necessary and the right things will come at the right time and in the right place

+ always concentrate on the ideal, he says, as an already existing fact, as he suggests that this is a "cell", the life principle which goes with faith and enters in and becomes set in motion, those causes which guide, direct and bring about necessary relation, which eventually manifests in form

Ralph Waldo Trine was a philosopher, mystic, teacher, author and early mentor of the New Thought movement

+ see yourself in prosperity and affirm for yourself you will be in prosperity, quietly, strongly, confidently. Believe it absolutely. Expect it, thereby making yourself a magnet

+ he speaks about a mind always hopeful, confident, courageous and determined on its purpose and keeping itself to that purpose, attracts to itself out of the elements, things and powers favourable to that purpose. He suggests to determine resolutely, to expect only what you desire, then you will attract only what you wish for and not to have a contradiction of wanting, but thinking of not getting.

+ see the good in everyone and appreciate it (not anything other than good). (From his book, 'In Tune with the Infinite').

Judge Troward was an English author who influenced New Thought, a divisional Judge in British administered India. He was also Her Majesty's Assistant Commissioner

+ had only one pupil, Genevieve Behhrend, who wrote the book, "Attaining Your Heart's Desires"

+ she suggests to stave off unwanted, negative, anxious thoughts and to keep a positive attitude of mind regarding your innermost desires as an accomplished fact, whether it be for a state of mind or for a thing

+ it is your intention that counts. The ALL-KNOWING POWER THAT IS understands and rewards accordingly

+ mentally picture yourself as doing the things that you enjoy, see yourself happy and lift your mind up to it by constantly repeating a happy affirmation and you will readily realise the reaction in kind

+ 'Attaining Your Desires' was a re-written version by Joe Vitale, because G Behhrend's version had so much influenced him.

H Emilie Cady was an American homeopathic physician and author of New Thought spiritual writings

+ suggests that with spiritual understanding comes new light on the scriptures. You will no longer run to and fro, seeking teachers or healers and rely solely on them, because you <u>will know</u> the living light, word within

+ be still, learn I AM, work within us so that we may have the mind of Christ and letting the I AM work itself. (From her book, 'Lessons in Truth').

James Allen was a British philosophical writer of inspirational books and poetry

+ is mostly known for his book, 'As a Man Thinketh'

+ a book about the power and right application of thought, in other words, it is suggested that Man is the Creator and Shaper of his destiny by the thought he thinks

+ we are given to understand that our personal environment is the result of what we have thought and that our future is being shaped and built by our desires, aspirations, thoughts and actions
+ by your attitude of mind, you are strengthening what is!

Chapter Four

Snippets of Spirituality

The Sages of Sivana

- were wise men from the Himalayas
- their secret of happiness is to find out what you truly love to do and then direct all your energy towards doing it
- be patient and live with the knowledge that all you are searching for is certain to come, if you prepare for it and expect it
- opposition thinking, when an undesirable thought occupies your mind, immediately replace it with an up-lifting one. In other words, whenever a negative thought comes up, replace it with a positive thought

- keep passion in the forefront of your mind, as you follow your mission and attain your goals
- enjoy the process with laughter and love

Eckhart Tolle, Author

- he reminds us of a quote from the Bible "Be still and know that I AM God"
- in his book, "A New Earth", he suggests 'being' is found in the still, alert presence of consciousness itself, the consciousness that you are
- he offers the secret of happiness as three words, "One with Life" - when you become aligned with whole, as a result, spontaneous, helpful occurrences, chance encounters, coincidences and synchronistic events happen.
- he mentions that whenever there is inspiration (which translates, 'in sprit') and enthusiasm (which translates, 'in God') there is a creative empowerment that goes far beyond what a mere person is capable of

Patty Harpenau

- wrote the book "The Life Codes"
- her web-page quotes "Happiness is an Inside Job"

- about wisdom of the heart, ancient knowledge passed down of teachings of Abraham (from the Bible) verbally from teacher to student and she obtained it from Rabbi Abraham
- about 7 spiritual laws which need to be experienced

  + law of unity (The God Code)
  + law of duality (The Adam Code)
  + law of desire (The Eve Code)
  + law of forgiveness (The Jeshua Code)
  + law of love (The Miriam Code)
  + law of trust (The Moses Code)
  + law of abundance (The Abraham Code)

- we are advised that everything is connected and within the code
- advised to pretend what we want is already there
- it is offered in the book, that which you want, you find by 'being' it
- everything already is
- the heart has a will of its own
- apparently, Mary said to Jesus, growing up, "Wherever you are, whatever you need, close your eyes and <u>feel</u> that what you need <u>is already present in your heart</u>"
- power of love

- the power of feeling with which you determine what you wish to see in life, when you are able to experience this feeling, as if it is already there, then it will appear
- how do we become all that we desire

  + by 'being' it
  + imagine what it would feel like and hold it close to your heart
  + it will begin to live within you.
  + you already are everything, everything already is and with the power of your thoughts, you make visible what before was hidden. With the power of your thought, you attract energy to you by what you think and feel
  + develop capacity of imagination, as the most powerful tool a person has is the ability to imagine things. You are where your thoughts are

- suggests that 'I AM that I AM' is that which you feel you become
- in the 'NOW', is the 'door' to the field of abundance.
- she learns that when we are in the 'NOW', we are where we plant our desire

- she is taught that gratitude brings the fulfilment of our desires
- also learns that 'Amen' is a code word, which means 'so be it', which is a law

  + in other words, we are given to understand we are certain and live in complete trust that you are making the connection

- apparently, Tibetans imagine the safe return of all their loved ones, as a sign of farewell
- Que Sabe means 'the One who knows'

Maitreya

- also known as 'Happy Buddha'
- says that laughter is sacred
- asks us to laugh more
- when we laugh, we are most connected to the Infinite, because the breath emitted through laughter <u>is</u> the <u>Allness</u>
- on his web-site, '<u>maitreya.org</u>', there is a message for humanity and their leaders

+ a request to be responsible
+ also, an explanation of different religions and order of them - 7 on the Great Sign (I understand that in Bible language the number 7 means complete)
+ they came in a certain order according to man's evolved understanding
+ each religion is complimentary to the other (see YouTube 'THOTH is the book with the seven seals (The Great Sign)'
+ he mentions ample supplies and life in space and the universe (mentioned in Sept 2014 Newsbrief)

– his message is "The Goal of the Life is to Be(come) Divine"

Chapter Five

Law of Attraction

A Universal Law that 'like attracts like' - so your feelings and thoughts attract similar into your life, be they positive or negative

Rhonda Byrne, Television Writer, Producer and Author

- wrote the New Thought book, "The Secret", also produced a film by the same name
- suggests that thoughts become things
- she suggests to see yourself living in abundance
- just think about things you want, not what you don't want
- asks us to keep with the 'good' feelings, as you get what you are feeling

- in other words, the universe will correspond and manifest like
- your thoughts and feelings will create your life
- do feel good more!

Diana Cooper, Author

- wrote the book "A Little Light on the Spiritual Laws"
- she suggests that we emit vibration which is made up of conscious and unconscious energy
- the underlying law is 'like attracts like' - our underlying beliefs attract situations and people to us
- likens us to a magnet, when we attract like to ourselves
- reminds me that it was apparently Prentice Mulford, back in the 1800s, who coined the phrase 'Law of Attraction'

Esther and Jerry Hicks, (Esther, Inspirational Speaker, Author and Jerry, Author)

- wrote a book called "The Law of Attraction"
- Esther Hicks receives inspirational messages of joy and well-being from 'Abraham' - a name given by a group of non-physical teachers
- we are given to understand that the Law of Attraction is the most powerful Law in the Universe!

- it is the basis of everything that we see manifesting, the basis of all things that come into our experience
- 'Abraham' defines Law of Attraction as "That which is like unto itself, is drawn"
- in other words, "that which you give thought to is that which you begin to invite into your experience"

Chapter Six

Channelling

Neale Donald Walsch channelled God

- Neale Donald Walsch channelled God through his writings
- from Neale Donald Walsch's book, 'Home with God', we are given to understand that we seek to re-create ourselves anew, like all of life, we will move more into the spiritual realm, in which we will come to know and understand more of Who You Are.
- this reminds me of the Greek aphorism "Know Thyself"
- also, it is mentioned that belief creates perspective
- 'Heaven' is getting what you want and 'Hell' is getting what you don't want! Hell is only created by

yourself, which can disappear the moment you don't want it, that is, when you want Heaven

- In Neale's book, 'The Holy Experience', it is mentioned that concerning 'happiness', and how to affect others, is not to the exclusion of yourself.
- In Neale's book, 'The New Revelations', the idea is offered - changing belief

    + it speaks of 'change' - that is, that it doesn't begin by trying to change the world, (I understand, we change ourselves and by doing so, have the effect of changing our 'outside' world)
    + again, I am reminded of the message at the end of the 'Bible Code' book, the idea/message, 'Will we change?'

- Neale asks God what is the difference between religion and spirituality? To which God replies that one is an institution and one is an experience
- God tells Neale that happiness and freedom is <u>not</u> being dependent upon another for your good
- God says do what makes you happy

- God advises to "be subjective" and do what we <u>feel</u> like doing!
- suggested by God that 'To Know Who You Are', a child of God, who was created to create good, the beautiful and the holy and that we are not to lose sight of this

Helen Schucman channels Jesus

- Helen Schucman channelled Jesus, hearing a 'voice' as she wrote
- Helen Schucman along with Bill Thetford, produced a book called 'A Course in Miracles'
- Jesus says that as you perceive, so shall you behave
- Jesus says that as you perceive it, believe it, live it

Esther Hicks channels 'Abraham'

- Esther Hicks is able to relax her conscious mind and allow the reception of Non-Physical answers to whatever is asked
- (the Non-Physical language is one of vibration)
- Esther and her Husband, Jerry, wrote, among many, the book, 'Ask and it is Given", which was 'dictated' through her by the Non-Physical Beings 'Abraham'
- they, that is Abraham, want us human beings to understand the <u>power of feeling good now</u> no matter

what and when we do, we will hold the **key** to the **state of being** and state of health, wealth, or state of anything that we desire!

— we are taught that we and everything are/is <u>vibrational</u> and that we are the creator of our own reality/experience and our 'power' is in the **'now'**

— emotions guide us in this, let them be our guide

— we are reminded that there is nothing that we cannot be, do or have! It's a case of putting oneself in a vibrational place of receiving all that we are asking for

— we get what we think about, whether we want it or not. We get whatever we put our attention to. We invite things through our thoughts

— to create that which we want, involves three 'steps':-

1. Ask
2. The answer is automatically given
3. The answer must be 'allowed' by you (you have to let it in!)

+ in other words, to allow and receive, <u>feel</u> good in the knowing that it is done and on its way!

— feel good emotions, be such ones as appreciation/ love, joy, ease, clarity, harmony

+ so when you are in a state of joy, happiness or appreciation, you are fully 'connected' to the stream of pure, Source energy
+ so it helps to keep reaching for the best-feeling thought you can - which creates best feelings

- 'Abraham' tells us to be present in the moment, is 'deliberate' creation and that our attention to anything, you get more of it!
- do not focus on lack of or not having, otherwise, that is what you will get!
- look for things to appreciate, to help <u>be</u> in the 'receiving' mode

  + appreciation is the fastest and easiest way!

- if you find yourself leaning towards negative things/ thoughts, start thinking "wouldn't it be nice if"
- Esther Hicks has very many 'YouTube' sessions, where she is recorded, channelling 'Abraham'. They are extremely fascinating and helpful. She is asked numerous questions by different members of the public. She spontaneously replies with very enlightening, up-lifting answers given through her by 'Abraham'-a YouTube session, "Abraham

Hicks session Depth of the Vortex", is a very good description and analysis of focusing on solutions to problems and what you want, rather than problems and on what you don't want

+ in other words, we are advised to be 'solution-based' not 'problem-based'
+ I am reminded of 'Course in Miracles', where part of the content from Jesus, channelled through Helen Schucman, tells us just the same, to focus on asking for solutions, not focus on the problem!

– in another YouTube session, "Abraham Hicks 2015 03 21 Fort Lauderdale Fl Session 1", Abraham, through Esther, advises us to "Get Happy" - which is the best place to 'be' for manifestation of good things, solutions and thoughts!

Darryl Anka channels 'Bashar'

– Darryl Anka is a Film Director and involved with special effects and model making for films. He has been involved in films such as Star Trek, Pirates of the Caribbean, the Aviator to name but a few. He had his own 'encounter' with sightings of a UFO a good number of years ago, which apparently turned out to be Bashar's craft - an equilateral triangle shape.

– Darryl becomes in an altered state of consciousness, where he feels energy and emotions but does not really hear the words. This allows the frequency of 'Bashar's' consciousness to impress itself upon Darryl's energy, thus creating a telepathic link between them. So concepts Bashar sends with his thoughts are automatically translated by Darryl's subconscious into whatever language Darryl is comfortable and familiar with. Bashar is described as 'Extraterrestrial'.

– Bashar's main message is "Follow your excitement"

+ says it is of "paramount importance"

+ tells us that vibration of excitement is vibrational resonance of our true, core, natural being

+ highest degree of excitement, act on your joy - this is Who I Am

+ the YouTube session "Bashar Finding and Following Your Excitement" is very good advice / explanation of 'Follow your excitement'

+ In other words, choose the one thing that has the highest amount of excitement to you and continue, taking action
+ he says "excitement is the thread that leads to all other excitement"

– the energy that leads you to yourself, the universe will support you. He describes it like the engine that drives all good things in your life
– in the book, 'BASHAR: Blueprint for Change. A Message from our Future", written by Darryl Anka and channelled by Bashar, Darryl points out that we are to "trust that the thing in life that excites you the most comes complete with all the tools necessary to support you in the doing of that thing. It is automatic; it is built in. All you need to do is act on the opportunities that doing that situation brings to you".

+ in other words, it is simply, "see, feel and be"

– see what you want
– feel it
– know it
– then be it

- <u>act</u> it (act as though you already have it,)
- teaches us about abundance, "<u>the ability to do what you need to do, when you need to do it</u>" as is said in the YouTube session, "Bashar on Abundance and Trusting What is"
- he says the more we enjoy the process, the faster it will go
- Bashar also teaches us that "circumstances don't matter, only state of <u>being</u> matters"
- state of being determines state of circumstances

   + in other words, to be in a state of gratitude, appreciation, joy, happiness, which will affect/connect to good situation, people, circumstances
   + we are advised to not be concerned about the 'how' things will happen, just trust that the universe will take care of it for you
   + Bashar tells us to believe before you see, <u>not</u> that 'seeing is believing'. Rather, believe you will see it

- Bashar advises us not to focus on our reality as it is
- just act/pretend/expect that it has changed, as you would rather it be and it will be

  + reminds me, the Abraham Hicks teachings tell us that same thing, pretend/imagine it has already happened and act as if it has and circumstances will begin to reflect this

- incidentally, there is a website, 'iasos.com', where there are clear explanations/instructions of 'Bashar's teachings, given by 'Elan', channelled by Andrew Bayuk, 'Elan' being another extra-terrestrial from the same Essassani civilisation
- interestingly, Bashar mentions in his teachings, the word 'IMAGINATION'. (YouTube session 'Bashar - Imagination - Zero Point). He says if we can imagine something, it is possible. He breaks down the word, I, MAGI, NATION and suggests that we are a nation of magi. Magi being magic as in wisdom. (Apparently, the three wise men in the story of baby Jesus, were known as Magi)

  + speaking of magic, I have just finished reading a book titled 'Nothing is Impossible' by 'Dynamo', who is known as 'the magician impossible!', who says that we are Creators of our reality and suggests that "nothing is impossible"! (This makes me think that the Bible tells us that "with God, all things are possible") 'Dynamo' seems to have discovered that if we can "imagine it, then it must be possible".

Other Channellings of interest

Robin Williams channelled by Laura M (seen on YouTube)
Robin Williams channelled by Meline Portia Lafont (seen on YouTube)
'Abraham' comments on Robin Williams (seen on YouTube - Abraham - Robin Williams)

Chapter Seven

Simple Physics

Nassim Haramein

–   Is a Director of Research for The Resonance
    Project Foundation, which he founded, who leads
    physicists, electrical engineers, mathematicians
    and other scientists. From the age of 9 years old,
    Nassim's lifelong vision is of applied unified physics
    to create positive change in the world. His most
    recent developments in quantum gravity and their
    applications to technology, new energy research,
    applied resonance, life sciences, permaculture and
    consciousness studies. He has made his own personal,
    independent study into physics, geometry, chemistry,
    biology, consciousness, archeology and various world

religions. As far as I understand, (at the time of writing) he is involved in getting a film organised called 'The Connected Universe'. He suggests that geometry connects the Universe.

+ I am very impressed with his individual work, that for me, ties up/marries up with 'simple physics' that 'Bashar' speaks about. Bashar says "the tetrahedron is the most basic fundamental form of manifestation in third density that you can have in physical reality." Nassim mentions that God's name YHWH, is a tetrahedron. YHWH or Yahweh, means 'causes to become'. It is interesting that Nassim's knowledge of 'science' meets with the world of spirituality, ie Bashar, very well. I would go so far as to say that it would be a truly wonderful thing if Nassim would be able to ask Bashar questions and to be able to hear answers from an extra-terrestrial! When this book is published, I will endeavour to get a copy of this book to both Darryl Anka and Nassim Haramein, suggesting this idea!)

'Bashar'

- Bashar speaks of 'electro-magnetism', in the book 'BASHAR: Blueprint for Change'. He says "all the power you need, all the technology you can invent, can be based upon electro-magnetic or granitic principles". "From that point on you will no longer create any toxic or radioactive by-products." He thinks that certain individuals on this planet, who are exploring and experimenting with certain types of molecular arrangements on polymers that stimulate certain biochemical processes in the body, certain biochemical arrangements in our human bodies within the DNA and RNA structures are closest to the mark where by a "new polarised particle" will be harmless to humans, "in a sense, it will be pollution of another type not harmful to humans"

- interestingly, in this book, Bashar explains Holy Spirit as "the collective electromagnetic mentality, the actual energy out of which all of your individual minds are created". It is "an electrical phenomenon, an electromagnetic phenomenon". He suggests that when we align with it in the vibration of excitement, service, positivity, you become of spirit and then we flow in harmony with all other beings, telepathically linked - more precisely, telempathy - emotionally activated by love, which is what he says the Holy Spirit is.

+ interestingly, Abraham Hicks teach that our emotions are our guides to help us keep connected positively to our heart's desires

— Bashar mentions that their 'starships' use electromagnetic energy, so they don't have to worry about rocket flames and fuel! Apparently, the 'ships' create a particular type of vibration that puts them out of phase with solid matter, so they can go into that solid matter or through it, or into other dimensions within it.

— Bashar says in a Youtube session, 'Bashar - Imagination -Zero Point', that when using your imagination, this is connecting with your Higher Self to enable your Higher Self to produce manifestations of your heart's desires. (There are many Youtube sessions of Bashar/Darryl Anka)

— In a YouTube session, 'DARRYL ANKA:CHANNEL FOR BASHAR', Darryl Anka speaks very openly, clearly and precisely about what he knows from Bashar about ETs and their knowledge and hopes.

Dr Joe Dispenza

– Dr Joe Dispenza is a researcher, neuroscientist, chiropractor, lecturer and author. He has been exploring how people can use the latest findings of neuroscience and quantum physics to heal illness and enjoy a more fulfilled and happy life. He has a creative approach which bridges the gap between neuroscience and true human potential. He explains how you can literally 're-wire' your brain to create a new mind and create new results in your life. It's an interesting, scientific approach which corresponds to the teachings of 'Bashar' and 'Abraham', alongside the law of attraction. In a YouTube session, he suggests that once in the now/present moment, when detached from past thoughts and feelings, you can use present, positive thoughts and feelings to create your future. He suggests that our personality creates our personal reality. In a talk in a YouTube session 'Breaking the Habit of Being Yourself - Introductory Lecture', Dr Joe suggests a choice of "we can learn and change in a state of pain and suffering or we can learn and change in a state of joy and inspiration". Also, the thought messages seem to me to be not unlike the New Thought writings of times gone by.

– through a study of people who had made a recovery called spontaneous remission, Dr Joe Dispenza discovered that it appeared these peoples' thoughts influenced their recovery, by deciding that they would change their way of thinking about themselves, by discarding 'old' thoughts and feelings and having new, positive, healthy thoughts and feelings about themselves, thus they became a 'new', 'better', 'healthier' person.

– Dr Joe Dispenza suggests that the frontal lobe of our brain "gives us permission to make thought more real than anything else." In other words, independent of time and circumstance. He says "thoughts matter".

– he suggests that our thoughts and feelings can contribute to disease, therefore, if we change our thought patterns by changing our thinking and thus our feelings, we "create a state of being". Therefore, if we believe before we see. (I can't help but think of Bashar's teaching - believing is seeing - rather than seeing is believing).

- the YouTube session, "Joe Dispenza - Your Immortal Brain - Mastering the Art of Observation", describes the above idea very well. In it, there is a conclusion that if we merge our minds with the greater mind and move our attention away from the environment, body, pure mind had a direct effect on physical body and nature of reality and matter. (I can't help but think of Abraham Hicks teachings that tell us to focus on what we <u>do</u> want and <u>not</u> on what we don't want!)

- Dr Joe Dispenza has written a book, "The Science of changing your Mind". Incidentally, I can't help but think of the question at the end of The Bible Code book, we are left with, about the idea, will we change? I am thinking this could well be about changing our mind!

- Dr Joe says we have three brains which allow us to go from thinking, to doing, to being and that to modify our behaviour creates new experiences. "State of being is when mind and body are working together" or "mind and body are one". He says that "universal principle says that everything responds to who we are being". He suggests that by modifying our behaviour by breaking the habit of our 'old self' and re-inventing our 'new self'. I am reminded that Bashar said that a habit is a belief you keep thinking! – Dr Joe even mentions 'Know Thyself', which he describes as to become aware of unconscious programs, have a level of awareness, self-honesty and to learn change in a state of joy and inspiration (rather than in something not healthy and not serving you, like pain and suffering). He suggests that our brain does not know if according to our thoughts, the situation is real or not. The idea is that we can decide to have thoughts different to circumstance that prepare us for new experience. This reminds me of both Abraham and Bashar's teachings. Abraham say that 'words don't teach, experience teaches' - which, incidentally, is a similar message in The Course in Miracles - while Bashar says 'circumstances don't matter, state of being matters'. Dr Joe says people are "missing the moment" by either living in the past or the future with their thoughts and emotion. In other words, being present, as energy in the heart, which he says "is a scientific, physiological phenomenon" - a state of joy and inspiration - a natural state of being - the person is a "no-body, no thing", which is something Bashar describes, as I understand. Dr Joe mentions that our "personality creates our reality", which reminds me of the Law of Attraction. He mentions to change our brain and body will change our experience. In other words, he says that if we change how we feel inside of ourselves, rather than the environment change our way of thinking - which reminds me of the Gnostics, when they say that the Kingdom of God is within you and spiritual laws, like, 'as within, so without'. Dr Joe even says we have to "trust in the unseen", "can we believe in a future that we can't see with our senses yet?" This reminds me that Bashar says that believing is seeing. In other words, believe what we see in our imagination with our thoughts and emotions, rather than believing what we see in our reality. He says to have a knowing that this will happen. I am reminded of the Gnostics, who said just the same, which is what they are meaning by "know thyself". Dr Joe Dispenza even suggests that to be happy, stop being not happy! This, to me, is a case of changing your mind and choosing a state of being. He even suggests that all the brain needs is clear understanding of our intention of our wants and desires and that we trust that these things come, which to me is what Abraham and the Law of

Attraction teaches and is about. Dr Joe says of us to open our heart and feel that it is so. His definition of enlightenment is "know that you know". This again makes me think of "Know Thyself". To me, in other words, by putting these thoughts and emotions into practice, it is done and will be, which reminds me of the word, Amen, meaning, so be it. He even says that emotions are energy in motion, which is exactly what Bashar has said. Dr Joe suggests that it would be interesting for people to see if they can change, by changing their thoughts and feelings.

— as a matter of fact, whilst writing this section of the book, I happened to come across writings by Neville Goddard, an influential New Thought teacher (of around the 1950s and 1960s), who seems to have this message of using your imagination to inspire your reality. In Neville Goddard's book, 'Seedtime and Harvest', there are real-time experiences of people who used their imagination to 'cure' themselves. They imagine a better body or re-enact an accident whereby there is a better, improved scenario. Also, in this same book, Neville Goddard offers the idea using a theme, the 'Four Mighty Ones of our imagination', whereby you are a Producer, Author, Director and Actor and using your imagination, play out as you would like a situation to to be. From Neville Goddard's book, 'The Law and the Promise', he says "Live as though the wish had come, even though it is yet to come and you will shorten the period of waiting." "The world is imagined, not mechanistic". Also, he says, "we must BE the state to experience the state".

— Fascinatingly, there is a YouTube session, 'Bashar : Imagination: Zero Point', where Bashar explains that our imagination changes our brain. He says imagination is the key to the Higher Mind, which allows alignment. He suggests that imagination is a state of being that causes changes in the neurology of our brain. He says "the way the electrical pathways flow will be different than any other state".

Chapter Eight

Friendly Aliens are waiting for our Welcome!

From Roswell Crash to Reverse Engineering

- Roswell Crash happened in mid 1947. Roswell, a town in New Mexico. US Military initially told the press that a "flying disc" had crashed, then subsequently said that it was merely a weather balloon. Around the 1970s, ufologists began the idea that one or more alien spacecraft had crash-landed and extra-terrestrial occupants had been recovered by the military who had engaged in a cover-up. On the Wikipedia website for the Roswell Crash, there is a copy of a United States Government letter to the Director, FBI, dated

Mar 22, 1950, from Guy Hottel (a special agent in charge of FBI's Washington Field Office), with the subject, "Flying Saucers". Part of the document reads, "According to Mr .... informant, the saucers were found in New Mexico due to the fact that the Government has a very high-powered radar set-up in that area and it is believed the radar interferes with the controlling mechanism of the saucers."

– Incidentally, in the book, 'BASHAR: Blueprint for Change', Bashar comments, under a chapter called 'UFOs Identified', about a UFO crash, "in July of" our "year 1947", Bashar says that "radar installation at that time had the ability to interfere with navigational guidance systems of those craft - although this is no longer true now. In interfering with the guidance systems, in altering the shape of the protective field around the craft, it created portions of the metallic hull of the craft to be vulnerable to the electrical storm; it was struck and knocked out, then recovered and retrieved by your government." He even goes so far as saying that "That particular craft is still in pieces under surveillance in many different areas of your country - but primarily near the area of Virginia." He says there were beings aboard.

- very interestingly, in Darryl Anka's book, 'BASHAR: Blueprint for Change. A Message from our Future', Bashar states "The Governmental structures you have created on your planet (book fourth printing, January, 1997, first printing, October 1990) are still insisting we do not exist and therefore we cannot violate that chosen belief." "Do understand that your government is very well aware of our existence - very well aware." He goes on to say that "There has been actual physical interactions between members of our society and your government". Bashar says that they (from Essassini) desire that our world and their world "shall one day soon explore together all that exists in the Infinite Creation" as they "already do with many civilisations." He suggests that when, as a group, we can determine that they can interact as equals, they "will then do just that."

- In the YouTube session, 'Bashar - Phoenix Lights', Bashar says we "are surrounded by alien beings on "our very own planet". He mentions 'Phoenix Lights' (an incident which was a UFOS sighting in Phoenix, Arizona and Sonora, Mexico, 13 March 1997) and says "the ship involved in that display is of the civilisation contacting you first, the ship, more than a Mile long passed over an entire state, many cities, witnessed by thousands of humans to gauge your response, your reactions and to awaken those who are ready to be awakened to themselves and to others. More such occurrences will happen after the response to that one has been fully gauged." He suggests that "when more of those occurrences unfold in your years between 2010 - 2017 there will be opportunity like never before for each and everyone of you that are willing, that are of a mind to, to become more active in laying down groundwork socially, politically, for the idea of avenues that will be more conducive to creating open contact between yourselves and other civilisations."

— In the YouTube session, 'Bashar - The UFO Witness Declaration Part 1 and Part 2', states facts about UFOs before a Declaration. (**This Declaration, as far as I can make out, is really a message for mankind! Bashar says to "post, send, spread this Declaration in its exact form, wherever you wish. It has been designed with a specific frequency, a specific vibration. Do not alter it. Do not paraphrase it. Do not add to it. Do not subtract from it. Send as is intact. It has a particular frequency that will** aid and assist in the acceleration of thus energy, this awareness, this awakening, of this state of being, in all those who are, at the very least, willing to be open to this information, willing to be open to this energy, willing to be open to the reality of contact between your civilisation, our civilisation and other civilisations for already observing, already present and despite what many individuals on your planet may believe, may think or may assume is possible or not possible, we exist, we know you exist. Travelling to your world is not so difficult as many as your scientists may think. They will soon come to understand how this is accomplished." He says our natural evolution of species is of "Homo Sapiens" to "Homo Galacticus"! (I leave the reader to choose for themselves whether to read this declaration and what they choose to decide about it. I will say, however, it is not something to be missed or ignored! As I say, it is your choice.)

— From the Roswell crash, has come reverse engineering. (Reverse engineering, whereby an object is taken apart to determine how it works, to enable duplication or enhancement of the object. It is a process of extracting knowledge, such as design information, in order to re-produce or produce something else based on the extracted information.). In 1997, Colonel Philip Corso, an American Army officer, who served in the US Army from 1942 to 1963, made a series of statements such that "the Roswell UFO crash did really happen, the craft was a biological spaceship that worked in conjunction with a crew of Extraterrestrial Biological Entities (EBEs) who drove it through a particular neural interface", as quoted from information on the 'Openminds.tv' website. He apparently executed orders from General Arthur Trudeau, at the Pentagon. He had responsibility for handling the recovered parts of the flying saucer to several US companies connected to the US Army in reverse engineering operation. (Again, information from the 'Openminds.tv' website.)

— The reverse engineering from the Roswell crash, it seems has come integrated circuits, night-vision technology, fibre optics, super tenacity fibres, lasers and cutting edge technologies. Such things are apparently written about in Corso's book, 'The Day after Roswell'. I have taken this information from the 'biblioteapleyades.net' website. (Interestingly, I believe Bashar made similar comments about us humans gaining this advanced knowledge in such a way and that the spaceships are run by the extraterrestrial's 'brain' by some form of telempathy, in either one of his many YouTube sessions or his book.)

– Incidentally, it is said there was a UFO crash, in Germany, back in the 1930s, whereby reverse engineering took place

– According to the book 'BASHAR:Blueprint for Change A Message from our Future', Bashar states "when your society allows itself to realise that all power you need, all the technology you can invent, can be based upon electromagnetic or granitic principles", he even goes on to say "From that point on you will no longer create any toxic or radio-active by-products".

– Interestingly, for all you scientists, in this same book, Bashar mentions a "black hole gate", which he describes through a physiological analogy, he says "imagine a ball of clear light, clear energy on the surface. As you sink slowly into it, it becomes white, white energy. As you go more toward the centre, it then condenses and collapses into a bright electric blue, electromagnetic energy. And at the very center

is what you would typically call a black hole gate".
He suggests that "projection and communication
with other civilisations through that black hole gate
at the very center of their world" would be "is an
interdimentional gate that links to all levels, all
dimensions and through which they" (the Sirius
civilisation) "can communicate on either directions -
with any level, any dimension".

— Apparently, a Don Phillips, was in the Air Force at Las
Vegas Air Force Base and witnessed (about 1966/67)
an event when UFOs were seen near Mt Charlotte,
North west of Las Vegas. According to him, (on
the ufology.wikia.com website) there are records and
filmed documentation of meetings in California in
1954 between Extraterrestrials and leaders of the
USA. He also lists a few of the technologies we were
able to develop because of the ETs: computer chips,
lasers, night vision, bullet proof vests. He speaks of
his experience of this UFO event, in the Youtube
session, 'Technology from Extraterrestials-Don
Phillips, USAF, Lockheed Skunkworks/Disclosure
Proj.Arch". In this interview, he speaks of Roswell
and says there were "captured craft" and that
technology was taken from them and was put to

work. He says "there was no question that there are people or beings from outside the planet that have lived here for a long time". He confirms that the Roswell crash was due to the guidance mechanism interrupted by the U.S. radar. Also, in this interview, he mentions that the 'beings' that 'piloted' the UFO, did so by "hands" and "their thought process", "their hands in rhythm with their thoughts". He says they "were trained to be one and use their being to flow with, to work with the natural forces of what we call the Universe". Amazingly, Don Phillips describes that the extraterrestrials helped electro-mechanics build a 'trainer' to enable us to learn to fly their type of craft!

–   A Dr Steven Greer, who has been an emergency room physician and ufologist has founded the Center for the Study of Extra-Terrrestrial Intelligence (CSETI) and has also founded The Disclosure Project, whose aims are to disclose to the public the government's (US) alleged knowledge of UFOs, extraterrestrial intelligence and advanced energy and propulsion systems. Dr Greer speaks of a "quantum vacuum", which, according to wikipedia.org is "fleeting electromagnetic waves and particles that pop into and out of existence". My understanding of his talks that I have seen on YouTube, is that he says that the extra-terrestrial entities are waiting for us to be ready to help ourselves and that they are concerned about our weapons and the threat of us destroying Earth and space. He speaks of the power of our mind and thought and says that consciousness is the key to communicating with ETs. He says they use "bio-electromagnetic field" and that they connect by mind. In the YouTube session, 'Dr Steven Greer "Time for Truth"', there is very revealing information and details of his experience and knowledge of ETs and military and government knowledge. In it, he also says that ETs are here to help us and they are not hostile! (He even suggests in his talks that if they were hostile they could have done away with us along time ago!). According to the website, 'disclosureproject. org', Dr Steven Greer has informed President Obama of knowledge and details relating to ETs and asks that this is investigated and made known to the public to enable a better form of energy, that ETs want to help us with, to be used instead of oil, gas, coal and nuclear energy. (He says that there has been a high level of secrecy concerning this, that they are very concerning and worryingly, U.S. Presidents have not been informed or dis-informed! (See the Obama Briefing Documents on this website.). (As I write this, I remember that 'Obama' was mentioned in the Bible Codes!). One document is a letter sent from Dr Greer to President Obama, dated January, 23, 2009, which explains fully and clearly the situation regarding ETs and new energy and suggestions of ways ahead.

– (As a matter of interest, a Lord Hill Norton, Admiral of the Fleet, Senior Royal Navy Officer (see YouTube 'Lord Hill Norton, Former NATO Head Tells the UFO reality (Audio only)' speaks of an 'Alien' encounter at RAF Bentwater, Suffolk, England and suggests we have and are being visited by "others" from other civilisations, which should be looked upon as a serious matter. He even wrote to Mr Heseltine, in 1985, to the then Defence Secretary, to express his feelings about this incident (of 1980), see website'newsbbc.co.uk/2/hi/UK/8202157.stm', as 'Minister warning 'UK Roswell'.

– Whilst writing this, a BBC1 Programme was aired on 28/6/2015, entitled David Attenborough Meets President Obama. They share their passion for nature and what can be done to protect the environment. Between them, they agree that there is a need, globally, to work together, as we are all connected. David Attenborough says he believes "generating and storing power from re-newable sources, we will make the problem of oil and coal and other carbon disappear because economically we will wish to use other methods."

Crop Circles and Communication

— Crop Circles, it appears, are of two types, in as much some are man-made, while others are, as I put it, 'of another origin'. They are magnificently displayed, in geometric patterns that are often described as 'sacred geometry'. There is a very fascinating filming of this 'craft' and a close-up of the intricate result of a crop circle in the YouTube session 'REAL UFOs Filmed Making CROP CIRCLES in Wiltshire, England, 07/27/10'. It is truly wonderful, the detail of fancy 'corn knots' amongst the 'artwork'.

— Barbara Lamb (a Marriage and Family therapist, Hypnotherapist and Regression Therapist), has made her own study of crop circles over 20 years or so. On her website, 'barbaralambmft.com', it suggests that these crop circles have "complex messages", "deliberately given to mankind by an off-planet intelligence", which even includes such things as "UFO propulsion systems, magnetic and anti-gravity technology" and it is mentioned "preparations for transformational energies coming to earth and affecting all life here". She gives a very revealing interview of her experiences about these on a 'UFO HUB', on a YouTube session, 'CROP CIRCLES'

— interestingly, it is suggested by professionals that regarding older civilisations way back in our history, that have ancient, carved stones, pyramids and so on, may well have been created by extra-terrestrials that were here before and left these as marks/symbols to show they were here, like in same manner crop circles seem to be.

— another interesting point is that on a YouTube session, 'Bashar' was once asked what would be a great thing he would like to do if living on Earth now. To which he replied he would like to create a huge picture in flowers on the ground that could be seen and appreciated from the air, in other words, by an aerial view. (Actually, really, crop circles can only truly be appreciated from the air as an aerial view!)

– speaking about communication with ETs, 'Bashar' suggests that if we learn to communicate with Dolphins, they will teach us much about the way we will be communicating with other civilisations that we will encounter. (This is from the book 'BASHAR:Blueprint for Change A Message from our Future'). In fact, he says that whales and dolphins are an alien civilisation in our own various oceans. He even goes so far as to say that "they have been in telepathic communication with many different civilisations off your planet for quite some time".

– in a BBC4 programme called 'The Girl Who Talked to Dolphins', it is mentioned that a Dr Lilly had funding from NASA for research in communication with Dolphins as they thought that was how we could communicate with aliens! It turned out that Dolphins couldn't speak our language, it was deduced that we need to learn theirs! This was back in the early 1960s.

– an extract from a web-site, 'thenewearth.org', '2 May 2014 Matthew Update from The Spiritual Realms on the 'World Situation', speaks about "Whales and Dolphins" comprising "the most highly evolved souls on the Planet intellectually and spiritually. They know your thoughts. They communicate telepathically with each other".

– another fascinating topic, is what is known as the 'Crystal Skulls', I understand there are 13 in total. 'Bashar' speaks about them in the YouTube session, 'Special Bashar with permission for the Crystal Skull a Conference', saying they were around as far back as 30,000 years ago from Atlantis culture and got transported to other locations around our planet where they were 'discovered'. He says some were created before Atlantean times, apparently by 13 masters, each created a master skull - "a collective energy". He says the number 13 in our society is regarded as a "transformational number" as it relates to a new "re-crystallised state", a "true neutralisation of reality", - "dimensional reality". The skulls "were carved in a variety of ways, but primarily a technique was used of vibration". The 13 masters got together to create certain sounds with their own bodies or certain instruments so crystalline would vibrate very rapidly which could be used as a tool to shape the master crystals by sound vibration through sonic vibration. They, that is the skulls, each have a unique "symbol" of qualities, such as "transformation", "expansion", "balance", "manifestation", representing qualities of each 'master'. Apparently, they are all 'connected' with one another, even now, albeit, somewhat 'weakened'

— in his book, 'BASHAR:Blueprint for Change A Message from our Future', Bashar describes 13 as "the transformational gate", a number which allows us to face all the different portions we have perhaps hidden from ourselves, segregating ourselves into and says it is why it is "transformational, magic number and why there is so much superstition associated with it in your society".

— Coincidentally, I have just come across "Solfeggo Frequencies" (see 'solawakening.com), which are apparently electro-magnetic frequencies. (My personal thought would be, is this what the crystalline skulls may have been about?). These frequencies are nine in total and made up an ancient tonal scale of chants and sacred music. They are said to be of three mathematical, geometric and frequency matrices which create the scale. By, apparently, exposing the mind and body to these particular frequencies, you can achieve a greater sense of balance and deep healing quite easily. They align you with rhythms and tones which form the basis of the Universe. Six electro-magnetic scales were rediscovered by a Dr Joseph Puleo in 1974. These scales are mentioned in entries from the original Apocrypha.

Chapter Nine

Hollow Earth, The Galactic Federation, Ashtar Command and Alaje

Hollow Earth

– apparently, it seems, that the planet Earth is hollow and it is suggested that advance civilisations exist there! According to different sources, there are 'openings' to it, the two largest openings being those found at the North and South Poles. According to the website, 'new-age-of-Aquarius.com', "on 23 Nov 1968, a very clear image of the hole at the North Pole was taken by the satellite ESSA-7". According to an account by a Norwegian sailor and his father (written by Willis George Emerson), they journeyed to Hollow Earth through the opening in the Arctic in 1829. They stayed there for approximately 2 years and returned to the surface of the Earth through an opening in the Antarctic

— also, an Admiral Richard E Byrd (an American Naval Officer who specialised in feats of exploration and was a pioneering aviator, polar explorer and organised polar logistics,) recorded his experience of visiting there, in his diary titled "The Inner Earth My Secret Diary".

— absolutely, amazingly, in the YouTube session 'Galactic Federation Update. Malaysian Flight370-**March 26, 2014,' the missing Malaysian passenger plane, is mentioned, saying that it's problem started to happen near a 'portal', when electrics/devices failed and behaved strangely and the pilots did not know what to do. This was around S E Asia, off coast of S Africa, S America and W Australia. It apparently 'recovered' and was "swept in Argatha", the Inner Earth, the Hollow Earth**

The Galactic Federation

- this Galactic Federation is "here to assist us during" our "ascension process" and that "Earth had been quarantined by the Galactic Federation of Light in order to curb the activities of the dark forces". They are extra-terrestrials and have, according to this website (new-age-of-Acquarius.com), disabled nuclear missiles and even mitigated the radiation emitted from from Japan nuclear crisis. (I can't help but remember what Dr Steven Greer has said along the same lines regarding their presence and intentions and concerns). On this website, there is a video showing UFOs over London, Friday, 2011. The Galactic Federation of Light, according to YouTube session 'Galactic Federation of Light (HQ)', have technology that is exceptionally advanced and have a profound understanding of consciousness and how to incorporate it into their technology. They can warp from place to place, time travel and teleport.

The Ashtar Command

- according to this same website, 'new-age-of-Aquarius.com', The Ashtar Command, is part of

The Galactic Federation and are working with the Ascended Masters under direction from The Galactic Federation, to achieve the divine mission of attending to Earth's affairs. They monitor major activities on Earth. They are Higher Beings which are known to be part of the Solar Star Command, who are Ashtar Sheran, Hatonn, Sananda Esu Immanuel and Vrillon. Sananda Esu Immanuel is Lord Jesus Christ. The Solar Star Command, or Ashtar Command, as it was known, has contacted Earth before, through their Vrillon, during 1977, when ITN TV evening news broadcast in England was disrupted. There is a transcript of their broadcast on this website, when the basic message is to warn our race on planet Earth regarding the use of nuclear energy and the wastes from atomic power and ask that we seek to know ourselves and live in harmony with the ways of planet Earth. You can watch and listen to this broadcast on the YouTube session,

'Original Vrillon message from 1977'.

– I once came across some information from Jesus, of the Ashtar Command, on the Internet, website, 'bibliotecapleyades.net', that said that we were to "Recognise but one race, the race of humanity - heavenly universal Man". He said that "Man, manifestation of the One". He said that "AN, Also Manas, the divine Mind or thinker and Human, God- man the one who can <u>know</u> the heavenly divine self". Also, "HU, an ancient word for God". He said that "ASH means Shepherd" and that "Ashtar is a code name for the one who overseas a commander, the administration fleets of the Most Radiant One - Sananda". He says that "ATHENA is counterpart energy... "wisdom.". "SherAn" .... "assist in redirecting and ascending planetary world from the involutionary codes 666, into those resurrected life eternal or 999, thereby re-splicing as it were, a planetary world <u>back</u> into the tree of life everlasting". ("The restoring of a world to the Divine Plan through Christ pattern".) He said that "lineage of AN or ON appears at the beginning and ending of major cycles as teachers of the Universal Law of Oneness," ("when one is in clear alignment with Source, one <u>becomes</u> a channel or conduit for the flow of greater divine empowerment". He said that "Adam Kadmon" ... "state of perfected Manhood".). He even mentions that they send us "messages of love and wisdom via crop circles or snow and ice circles. We also form messages within your skies. **These will continue and increase until your planet realizes that you are not alone, that you are loved and part of a plan more beautiful and wondrous than you could have ever imagined**"

— another entry, '23 Oct 13 Commander Ashtar on the coming changes - Elizabeth Trutwin', from the book, 'The New Earth Book II', on the website, 'thenewearth.org', Commander Ashtar describes there will be "Free energy, Replicators and Healing Machines", "Homes for the Homeless, clean water and communication technologies. Shuttle Craft to fly to the Light Cities. There will be little boxes, the size of a shoebox, which will be able to power your entire house for free". (Dr Steven Greer speaks of a similar thing that is ready now to produce, once 'Disclosure' is made and we, humankind is ready to be at peace with each other and extra-terrestrials)

— Also, there seems to be a new type of funding system that is being organised, headed by St Germaine, called NESARA (which stands for National Economic Security and Reformation Act), which is to benefit Mankind

- Very interestingly and amazingly, there is a message on YouTube from The Ashtar Command, 'Ashtar Malaysia Flight 370 March-12-2014 Galactic Federation of Light', which is channelled by a Dr Kathryn E May, whereby it is said to the effect that the passengers are all fine and happy to go along with the idea they are missing until Mankind come to realise that World Peace is needed. The message says they have their cell phones and if they want to return, they have their choice to do so. <u>The message says they are in Hollow Earth, I urge each reader of this book to listen to this message and make for themselves what they think.</u>

- Very interestingly, in the YouTube session, 'Aircrash Investigation 2015 What Happened to MH370 Malaysia Airlines Flight 370 Premiere', it is said that as far as technology can deduce, last known records are that the plane was headed for Antartica. In the YouTube session, 'BBC Documentary-Where is Flight MH370- Discovery Channel BBC Horizon', it states that last known records show the plane was over the Southern Indian Ocean.

- compare this with the website, 'bbc.co.uk, on News Asia, dated 30 Jan 15, titled, 'Missing Malaysia plane MH370:What we know', it says there was a request from the aircraft "to log on" which "investigators say is consistent with the plane's satellite communication equipment powering up after an outage - such as after an interruption to its electrical supply". (This, to me, matches up with The Galactic Command's comments about the plane's electric devices failing).

- (Also, I read somewhere on one of these YouTube messages, that apparently, the 'cigar-shaped UFO' seen over Ukraine is monitoring areas of conflict and can, as it were, de-activate our weapons, if need be to protect our planet!) (In the book, BASHAR: Blueprint for Change A Message from Our Future, there is a diagram of 'Solar Wind', the 'Mother Ship' (p216), which is described as being a mile long! I can't help but think that this could well be the 'cigar-shaped' UFO).

- At the website, whoneedslight.org, there are New Scriptures by Jesus/Sananda, transcribed by Kathryn E May, PsyD, (revised 2015), which is a very clear, personal autobiography, clearing his name and situation/reputation. He says "There is no hell other than the one you create in your minds". He explains, amongst many other things, his true relationship with Mary Magdalene, Judas and his life according to himself. I very much encourage you, dear reader, to take the time to read these 'writings' from Jesus. He mentions that the "Vatican officials have been steeped in centuries of secrecy and absolute financial power"...."which give the Church ownership of all the lands that have ever been held by the Crown of England......." He goes on to say that "the Catholic Church is the most powerful consolidated political force on the planet". He even goes on to say that "transportation over long distances will be accomplished by individual or community spaceship" and that our "Star Brothers and Sisters are circling" our "planet now to bring ...technologies, their knowledge and their help in fulfilling the Dream of Ascension". An absolutely revealing read!!

Alaje

– Alaje is from the Pleiades, as far as I can understand, in a human body. There is a powerful message from Alaje to us that is well worth listening to, where, basically, he says that love and wisdom equals spiritual energy and to become love and not fear. When more of us do thus, more of the "spiritual beings" will come to us, with their 'star ships' and why they, at the moment only contact spiritually 'happy' beings. He does seminars where he teaches "the meaning of life is the development of the heart and the consciousness" and "in order to get in a higher dimension, you have to be free of all negative energies". He also says "we have to learn to control our thoughts and our emotions, because this is creating the outside life", "it is really time to live TRUE LOVE". He summarises that "LOVE IS THE SOLUTION FOR EVERYTHING". He says if you are spiritual, you see humans on the planet as one family connected to our Earth and Universe and suggests that the solution of all problems is always a higher frequency and this is Love and Joy. He goes on to say "Focus on WHAT YOU WANT TO HAVE and don't focus on what you don't want to have". "You have to FEEL what you want to have". This message seems to tie in with Abraham Hicks and Bashar. Speaking of Bashar, in the YouTube session, 'Bashar Power of Positivity', he mentions that his 'ship' is over Cairo. Bashar has also mentioned that his 'ship' is also called 'The New Jerusalem' and is headed by Jesus and Ascended Masters, such as St Germaine. This seems to tie in with Alaje's message. — fascinatingly, I was once watching, I believe may have been a BBC documentary, I think was about some kind of history/religion and on the programme it was mentioned that near to Lullingstone Villa, which is in Kent, England (which are from Roman Times) is a early, Christian symbol which Christians would recognise one another. It is circular, with three 'symbols' on it, like the shape of a half-moon, which represents Cairo (the ancient spelling is CHIRHO, which is one of the earliest forms of Christogram and is form by superimposing the first two capital letters chi and rho (XP) of the Greek word XPETOE equals Christ, in such a easy to produce the monogram and invokes the crucifixion of Jesus as well as symbolising Christ. (Interestingly, the chi-rho, meaning 'good', was used by the Roman Emperor Constantine I, as part of a military standard). Back to the circular symbol, there is a marking that looks like a capital A, which means Alpha and a marking that looks a little like the letter W, which means omega. (Alpha-first, Omega- last). In the circle is a criss-cross with

5 points and the points are believing, perceiving, thinking, feeling and acting. These, for me, are truly fascinating, as they remind me of points mentioned by both Bashar and Abraham Hicks and being that CAIRO is mentioned, remembering that Bashar said himself his 'starship', 'The New Jerusalem', part headed by Jesus (known as Santanda Esu Immanuel) and spoken about by Alaje, is over Cairo

– on the website, '777ALAJE' (which is claimed to be the 'official' website), there is absolutely fascinating information about crop circles, where he speaks of them being made by 'energy' and even about the Greek gods, such as Hermes, as extra-terrestrials on Earth and how humans of the time depicted them with wings on feet, or on backs of heads, to show they came from another planet.

– the information from Alaje comes in YouTube videos, 'Alaje Padt 1 of 19 Pleiadian Message from The Galactic Federation (old version)' and others, where he says we are being kept in ignorance of extra-terrestrials, we need to do our own research and that their star "ships" are "consciousness" and that they "are flying with divine energy" and that they can appear in different form and as a "light", "transparent" or "invisible". There are films showing his "light" ships, one of which is filmed in Avebury, England at around about 2003, all filmed by himself. On one of his videos, he even says that the star of Bethlehem was only one of their light ships and that any mention in the Bible about clouds 'speaking', were their lightships. On the website, 'soundofheart. org', there is a video by Alaje about the secrets of Atlantis and gives an account of Atlantis and history before it. He did this when he visited Bimini, which he says is what is left of Atlantis, near the Bermuda Triangle.

– at the time of writing this section, I have come across the website, 'thenewearth.org', which seems to be a form of a history of Spiritual Hierachy and galactic history. For example, Feb 21, 2006 there is a description of Motherships, internal and their environments, May 23, 2006, a description of Inner Earth, topography, etc, April 10, 2007, mentions "back-engineered" technology from "downed space vehicles", June 5, 2007 and an entry dated 27/7/2005, where Barack Obama is mentioned as a "Light Being" and that "a powerful shield of Christed Light is keeping him one of the most securely protected persons on the planet". An entry dated August 8, 2008, says that "Free energy is the answer".

– in an entry dated 2 March 2010, the Galactic Federation Regional Council on Sirius B, proposes a mergeance of Agartha civilisation (being 5D realm) below Earth's crust, which it says has been around for about 13 millennia and Earth as we know it (3D realm). They plan for us to have "field trips" to visit their "Motherships". They "plan to share" their "ships and technology" with us. There is even suggestion that Mars has "vast underground technical facilities" which will "terraform" Mars into a Water World and likewise, Venus is being "readied to transform into a Water World" that we will get to visit

– an entry dated 28 Nov 2009, from a Lady Master Nada, speaks of President Obama as "The Siriun Commander" and a "Member on The Council of Nine on Sirius". He is apparently the Ninth member and she describes him as "a Galactic Human" who "has adept skills and abilities and spent the last 1000 lifetimes preparing for this life" and is "the Representative for what is known as Gaia Collective consciousness" and that "Sananda, Lady Master Nada and Barack Obama are working together in support roles". (I can't help think that no wonder Obama is mentioned in the Bible Codes!)

– on the same website, under "The New Earth Book 2", there is channelling of President K F Kennedy, by Susan Leland, which says that J F Kennedy was due to make a speech about 'friendly ETs' before he was assassinated. There is a copy of the speech that was never 'spoken' on the website. JF Kennedy says he went to the starship, "the New Jerusalem". (There is even an account of the assassination "Extracted from "The Phoenix Journals", No 51, by Hatonn/ Christ Michael). In this 'book', is a full description of the New Jerusalem Mothership. In fact there is a vast, truly incredible and fascinating account of all things developing in the 'spiritual/ETS world, that is so amazing, I think it is best left to you, the reader to choose, if you so wish, to read and make what you will of it. I am reminded of what Alaje has said, when he suggests we make our own journey of discovery!

I have certainly made my own journey of discovery and what a delightful, revealing, enlightening and encouraging journey it has been! SO WELL WORTH MY WHILE and amazingly, it is so simple, as Bashar and Abraham try to impress us, just BE HAPPY and all good things/people/ circumstances will come your way! (Don't wait to be happy, be happy in the moment, the NOW, knowing/expecting good things coming!)

So, it's over to you, reader, to make your own journey of discovery and as you hear Abraham say to us, so many times in their YouTube sessions, "words don't teach, experience teaches"! You have to have your very own, personal experience!

To end on a happy note, Bashar says "Be happy. You don't have to wait for a reason to be happy in order to know you prefer to be happy". He emphasises "Create the effect of being happy and you will attract into your lives all of the causes to support the happiness you have created". (From Darryl Anka's book, 'Bashar: Blueprint for Change. A Message from Our Future.)

There is a song called 'Don't worry, be happy'! (Sung by Bobby McFerrin).

Recently, (you can watch it on YouTube, 'Dalai Lama - 80th birthday speech at Glastonbury 2015') the Dalai Lama spoke about being happy, his message seems to be to take each day as a 'Happy' Birth Day! In other words, as far as I understand, the 'birth' of a new day, be happy!

In conclusion, dear reader, it seems to me, to <u>BE</u> HAPPY, therefore, I AM HAPPY! It's a case of be happy, anyway, then all else falls into place, heart's desires come. Keep enjoying myself, be in my excitement - any little thing at any possible moment! In other words, keep in joy, love, think of good things, clarity, ease, fun. Life is supposed to be fun! Keep thinking and believing, therefore perceiving you <u>have</u> what you want and it and better things come to be. (Focus on what you want, not on what you don't want). So, <u>be</u> happy in the moment, the NOW, the sacred 'Nill' point (nothing, no-thing point) that connects all good and the Universal Law of Attraction will attract good - thoughts become things, then synchronocities happen, such as good things, places and people. (Likewise, accept alien/ETs are here for our good - for advanced, better technologies for home, business, travel and economics!). I can actually say, in practicing this way of life I have experienced good, synchronistic things and circumstances! It's worth 'testing' it out for yourself - enjoy your very own personal journey!

(Talking about synchronocities, as I finished this 'summary', to write my manuscript on my IPad, the time read, 11:11, which, according to Doreen Virtue's (Doreen is an author, counsellor and lifelong clairvoyant who works with the angelic realm) website, 'angeltherapy. com', this pattern of numbers means "Keep your thoughts positive, because your thoughts are manifesting instantly into form. Focus upon your desires and not on your fears"!)

With love, joy, light, blessings and happiness!

Linda Shrimpton
Author

References

Author and Book

Michael Drosnin, The Bible Code, Bible Code III

Jim Pritchard, The Warrior Mind

Ross Heaven, The Spiritual Practices of the Ninja

Adeline Yen Mah, Chinese Cinderella

Neale Donald Walsch, When Everything Changes, Change Everything, Home With God, The Holy Experience, The New Revelations

Guy Ballard (Godfre Ray King - pen name), The I AM Disclosures

James F Twyman, The Moses Code

Mary Baker Eddy, The Spiritual Writings of Mary Baker Eddy

Prentice Mulford, The God in You (Chapter 4 Love Thyself)

Florence Scovel Shinn, The Writings of Florence Scovel Shinn

Charles Haanel, The Master Key System

Ralph Waldo Trine, In Tune with the Infinite

Genevieve Behhrend, Attaining Your Heart's Desires

H Emilie Cady, Lessons in Truth

James Allen, As a Man Thinketh

Eckhart Tolle, A New Earth

Patty Harpenau, The Life Codes

Rhonda Byrne, The Secret

Diana Cooper, A Little Light on the Spiritual Laws

Esther and Jerry Hicks, The Law of Attraction, Ask and it is Given

Helen Schucman and Bill Thetford, A Course in Miracles

Darryl Anka, BASHAR: Blueprint for Change. A Message from our Future

Dynamo, Nothing is Impossible

Dr Joe Dispenza, The Science of Changing Your Mind

Neville Goddard, Seedtime and Harvest, The Law and the Promise

Colonel Phillip Corso, The Day after Roswell

Admiral Richard E Byrd, The Inner Earth. My Secret Diary

Elizabeth Trutwin, The New Earth II

Websites

maitreya.org

iasos.com

bahaistudies.net

resonance.is/explore/nassim-Haramein

en.wikipedia.org/wiki/Roswell_UFO_incident

Openminds.tv

biblioteapleyades.net

ufology.wikia.com

wikipedia.org

disclosureproject.org

newsbbc.co.uk/2/hi/UK/8202157.stm

barbaralambmft.com

bibliotecapleyades.net

thenewearth.org, 2 May 2014 Matthew Update from The Spiritual Realms on the 'World Situation'

solawakening.com

new-age-of-Acquarius.com

bbc.co.uk on News Asia, dated 30 Jan 15 'Missing Malaysia plane MH370: What we Know

777ALAJE

soundofheart.org

whoneedslight.org

angeltherapy.com

YouTube

THOTH is the book with the seven seals (The Great Sign)

Abraham Hicks - Abraham Hicks session Depth of the Vortex

- Abraham Hicks 2015 03 21 Fort Lauderdale F1 Session 1

Bashar - Bashar Finding and Following Your Excitement

- Bashar on Abundance and Trusting What Is

- Bashar - Imagination - Zero Point

Robin Williams channelled by Laura M channelled by Meline Portia Lafont

Abraham - Robin Williams

Nassim Haramein

Darryl Anka: Channel for Bashar

Dr Joe Dispenza - Breaking the Habit of Being Yourself- Introductory Lecture

- Your Immortal Brain - Mastering the Art of Observation

Bashar - Phoenix Lights

- The UFO Witness Declaration Part 1 and Part 2

Technology from Extraterrestrials - Don Phillips, USAF, Lockheed Skunkworks/Disclosure Proj.Arch

Dr Steven Greer "Time for Truth"

Lord Hill Norton Former NATO Head Tells the UFO reality (Audio only)

REAL UFOs Filmed Making CROP CIRCLES in Wiltshire, England 07/27/10

CROP CIRCLES

Special Bashar with permission for the Crystal Skull a Conference

Galactic Federation Update, Malaysian Flight 370 - March 26, 2014

Galactic Federation of Light (HQ)

Original Vrillon message from 1977

Ashtar Malaysia a Flight 370 March-12-2014 Galactic Federation of Light

Aircrash Investigation 2015. What Happened to MH370 Malaysia Airlines Flight 370 Premiere

BBC Documentary-Where is Flight MH370-Discovery Channel BBC Horizon

Bashar Power of Positivity

Alaje Part 1 of 19 Pleiadian Message from The Galactic Federation (old version)

Dalai Lama - 80th birthday speech at Glastonbury 2015

Television Programmes

BBC1 David Attenborough Meets President Obama
(According to IPlayer, aired 28/6/15)

BBC4 The Girl Who Talked to Dolphins
(Aired 12 May 2015)

About the Author

LINDA SHRIMPTON had, from a very early age, an interest in religion and a fascination of life in Mesopotamia, Egyptians and hieroglyphics. Later in life, she delved into many subjects and more especially into spirituality, where she gained a more fuller, deeper knowledge and understanding.

She has worked in the field of education for almost 20 years

About the Book

Having taken a journey through many subject areas—such as philosophy, psychology, religion, martial arts, spirituality, channeling, law of attraction and the universal laws, physics, sacred geometry, neurology, UFOs, ETs, and the spiritual realm—with the idea of finding out how to be herself, the author shares what she personally discovered along the way, spiritually. Be a human being while being happy! Be happy!

Printed in the United States
By Bookmasters